The War Years
The Home Front

Brian Moses

Wayland

Titles in this series

The War Years: 1939–45
Wartime Cookbook

Picture acknowledgements:
AKG London 12 top, 20, 21 top; Camera Press 4, 39 top, 45 top; Imperial War Museum *cover, title page,* 5 top, 6 bottom, 7 top, 8, 9 both, 10, 11 both, 13, 14 both, 17 both, 19 bottom, 21 bottom, 22, 23 top, 24, 25 both, 27 top, 28, 29 both, 35 bottom, 36 bottom, 38, 40, 41 bottom, 42 bottom, 43, 44; Magnum Photos Inc *cover, centre inset,* 34, 37; Peter Newark's Historical Pictures cover, right inset, 12 bottom, 15 top, 18, 19 top, 39 bottom; Popperfoto 27 bottom; Range/Bettmann/UPI 35 top; Mr Carel Toms 30, 32, 33 both; The Wayland Picture Library *contents page,* 15 bottom. The artwork on page 30 was supplied by Malcolm Walker.

Cover: (bottom) Bomb damage.
(Top left to right) recruitment poster for the Women's Land Army; young children from the East End of London; evacuees being delivered to their foster parents in the countryside.
Title page: Young evacuees about to leave the city.
Contents page: Bomb damage in central London.

Series editor: Francesca Motisi
Book editor: Joanne Jessop
Designer: Malcolm Walker
Production controller: Carol Titchener

First published in 1995 by
Wayland (Publishers) Limited
61 Western Road
Hove, East Sussex, BN3 1JD
England

© Copyright 1995 Wayland (Publishers) Limited

British Library Cataloguing in Publication Data
Moses, Brian
   The War Years: The HomeFront
   I. Title II. Jessop, Joanne
   941.084

ISBN 0-7502-1610-7

Typeset by Kudos Editorial and Design Services
Printed and bound by B.P.C. Paulton Books, Great Britain

Contents

The Prospect of War

When Adolf Hitler became the leader of Germany in 1933, he promised to make the country powerful again and gain back the lands Germany had lost at the end of the First World War (1914–18). In preparation for this, Hitler built up the German army and ordered the factories to make more weapons.

In 1938, the German army invaded Austria and made that country part of Germany. The following year, the army went into Czechoslovakia and then threatened to attack Poland. Britain and France warned that there would be war if Hitler invaded Poland.

Adolf Hitler taking the salute from his troops at a march-past parade during the Festival of the Whole Nation in April 1939.

On 1 September 1939, Hitler's troops stormed into Poland. The British threatened war if Hitler did not withdraw his troops 'immediately'. A deadline for the Germans to withdraw their troops was set for 11 am on 3 September.

Everyone hoped that the government would find a way of avoiding war, but the deadline passed with no word from Hitler. At 11.15 am the British prime minister, Neville Chamberlain, announced on the radio, 'Britain is at war with Germany'. The Second World War had started. It was to last until 1945 and involve all the major world powers and most of the smaller nations in the fighting.

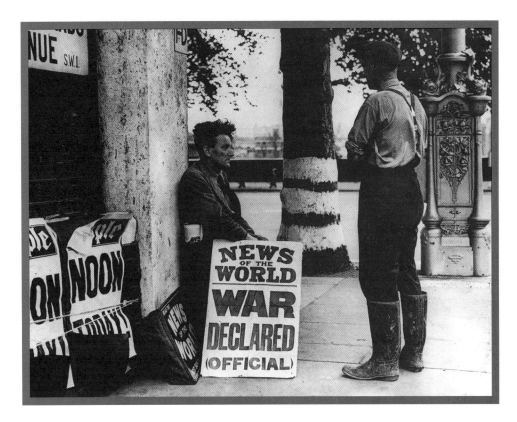

Left A newspaper seller in the streets of London on 3 September 1939, the day the Second World War broke out.

Below A recruiting poster for the Royal Air Force in the 1930s. Britain had been preparing for war long before it started.

It was on the 3rd – a pleasant, sunny Sunday morning – that we heard the fateful wireless announcement that a state of war existed between Germany and Britain . . . and almost immediately afterwards we were horrified to hear for the first time the dismal wailing of an air-raid siren. It was a false alarm, but initially terrifying.

The Day War Broke Out *by Peter Haining*

For many people, there were few immediate changes in their daily lives.

I suppose I was surprised that nothing seemed to have altered, now that we were actually at war. I don't think it entered our heads that some of us might get killed. But I know we were all of the same mind that day – that we must win.

The Day War Broke Out *by Peter Haining*

Preparing for War

These children are wearing their gas masks. This picture was taken in 1937 - the government handed out millions of gas masks even before the war broke out.

Below The first baby to be born in London after war was declared arriving home from the hospital in a gas-proof container.

Preparations for war began a few years before the war broke out. In the summer of 1938, the British government, fearing that the Germans would drop poison gas from aeroplanes, handed out over 40 million gas masks. They looked horrific, smelt of rubber and disinfectant, and were extremely uncomfortable to wear for more than a few minutes. Children under the age of two were to be placed in special gas-proof containers that could be supplied with filtered air by pumping hand bellows.

The government issued Anderson bomb shelters free to householders earning less than £250 per year. The Anderson shelter was made up of curved sheets of corrugated iron that were bolted together. These were dug into the earth and covered with soil.

6

Some people grew vegetables on top of the shelters, which led one journalist to comment that people were in greater danger of being hit by a marrow falling off the roof of an air raid shelter than of being struck by a German bomb.

Those people who had no garden in which to set up a bomb shelter tried to make a room in the home safe by sandbagging walls and boarding up windows. Or they may have used a cupboard under the stairs as a safe area. Others prepared to camp out in their basements.

Above Children clambering into an Anderson bomb shelter. The boy has his gas mask in the box hanging round his neck.

Once war was declared, there was a huge increase in volunteers who wanted to join the armed forces before their call up. Almost two million people volunteered to work for the Civil Defence services. They were taught about the dangers of air raids and told what precautions could be taken. Air raid wardens patrolled the streets in order to report bomb damages and alert rescue units.

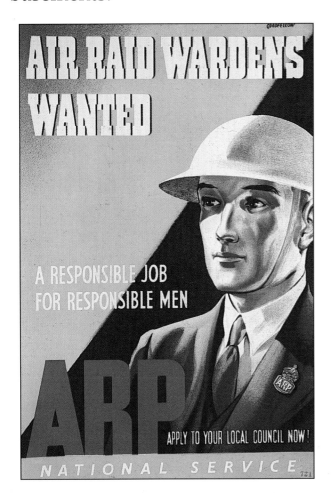

A recruitment poster for air raid wardens. Many women, as well as men, became air raid wardens.

7

Evacuation: Operation Pied Piper

I thought it was a Sunday-school outing down to the seaside, sort of thing. And I looked out of the bus window and I saw my mother crying outside and I said to my brother, 'What's Mummy crying for?' and my brother said, 'Shut up!'

No Time to Say Goodbye *by Ben Wicks*

In the spring of 1939, plans were drawn up to evacuate children from Britain's cities and ports. These were the places the Germans were most likely to bomb if war broke out. So the children from these areas were to be sent to live in the countryside where they would be safe.

Mothers and their young children at Victoria Station in London, 2 September 1939. They are leaving the city to live in safe areas in the countryside.

The evacuation plan, known as Operation Pied Piper, meant that children under five were evacuated with their mothers. Older children travelled with their teachers and then boarded out with foster parents. A householder who took in evacuees would be given 8 shillings and 6 pence (about 42p in today's money) per week per child.

Evacuation began on the day the Germans invaded Poland. About one and a half million women and children were evacuated during the next few days.

Left Chidren waiting to be evacuated by train.

Many children travelled on trains for most of the day, arriving dirty, hungry and exhausted. They were given something to eat while they waited to meet their foster parents for the first time.

We were told to sit quietly on the floor while the villagers and farmers' wives came to choose which children they wanted. I noticed boys of about twelve went very quickly – perhaps to help on the farm. Eventually only my friend Nancy and myself were left – two plain straight-haired little girls wearing glasses, now rather tearful. A large, happy-looking, middle-aged lady rushed in asking, 'Is that all you have left?' A sad slow nod of the head from our teacher. 'I'll take the poor bairns.' We were led out of the hall with this stranger and taken to a farm where we spent two years.

No Time to Say Goodbye *by Ben Wicks*

Below These mothers are close to tears watching their children leave.

9

Evacuation: New Lives

Many of the evacuees who came from the poorest parts of Britain's towns and cities were dirty and troubled by infections such as scabies. Often these children were not used to having baths or eating meals at a table. Their behaviour sometimes seemed like bad manners and shocked their foster parents. Two wartime children – Bernard Kops and his sister – who were evacuated from Stepney in London to Buckinghamshire, found the comforts of their new home quite strange.

Everything was so clean in the room. We were even given flannels and toothbrushes. We'd never cleaned our teeth up till then. And hot water came from the tap. And there was a lavatory upstairs. And carpets. And something called an eiderdown. And clean sheets. This was all very odd and rather scaring.

The World Is a Wedding *by Bernard Kops*

Mrs Annie Norris, a 67-year-old woman, took in six evacuee children.

Children being taught in the open air. With so many children moving to the countryside, there was a shortage of classroom space.

Sometimes it was the other way round, and evacuee children left homes in the city that had bathrooms and electric lights only to find themselves in farm cottages with no electricity or piped water.

For many evacuees this was the first time they had seen the countryside. They learnt about farms and animals and helped with the harvest. Some children were so happy in their new homes that they did not want to go back to the city.

British evacuee children waving a greeting to New York City in the USA, which was to be their new home during the war.

It was often hard for local children to accept the 'vackies'.

> *The village didn't know what hit them when we first arrived, it was gang warfare between us and the local kids. There wasn't a fruit tree within miles around with a single stem of fruit left on it. After a while things settled down to an uneasy truce.*
>
> No Time to Say Goodbye
> *by Ben Wicks*

Some children were evacuated overseas to the USA, Canada or Australia, but this came to a halt in September 1940 when a U-boat sank a ship and 73 'seavacuees' were drowned.

The Blackout

On 1 September 1939, it became illegal to allow any light to show from a building at night. Air raids were expected to take place during darkness, and if German bombers saw lights from the buildings below they would know exactly where to drop their bombs to do the most damage.

Blacking out windows became a nightly routine during the war.

During the blackout, people covered their doors and windows with heavy curtains, blinds or thick paper. Some even painted over their windows. There were no street lights, and cars and buses were fitted with masked headlights. Air-raid wardens reported blackout offences such as

UNTIL YOUR EYES GET USED TO THE DARKNESS, TAKE IT EASY

LOOK OUT IN THE BLACKOUT

This wartime poster reminded people to be careful during the blackout.

12

This woman is painting white stripes on a cow from an Essex farm. The farmer tried to protect his cows by painting white stripes on them to make them visible to motorists in the blackout.

letting light escape from the house when opening a door or striking a match in the street, and the guilty person was fined.

When the raids did not happen, people became increasingly annoyed by the blackout. Preparing for the blackout each night took time and became a nuisance. The dark streets made driving and getting about at night very dangerous; many people were killed in road accidents or drowned when they fell off bridges.

At the beginning of the blackout there were more casualties from road accidents than from enemy actions. White lines were painted along kerbs and men were encouraged to leave their white shirt tails hanging out at night. A local farmer painted white stripes on his cows in case they strayed on to the roads.
War Boy: A Country Childhood *by Michael Foreman*

However, when the German bombs started to fall in the summer of 1940, everyone worked even harder to enforce the blackout.

In Short Supply

At the beginning of the war, most of Britain's food was brought in by ship. Once the war started, the German navy tried to sink any ships bringing food to Britain. By January 1940, some foods were in short supply and had to be rationed. Every person in the country was given a ration book with coupons to be handed over to the shopkeeper when buying food. People registered with their local grocer and butcher and were not allowed to buy rationed food in any other shops. Shopkeepers had to sell rationed food at prices fixed by the government.

Above A shopkeeper marks up a ration book.

Below Hyde Park and Kensington Gardens became allotments.

One way to get extra food was to grow it. The government encouraged people to 'Dig for Victory'. Vegetables were planted in flower gardens, allotments and parks, and on roadside verges and railway embankments. Newspapers and magazines gave helpful tips on how to cook home-grown vegetables in unusual ways. There was even a recipe for carrot marmalade!

In June 1940, clothes rationing was introduced. Each person in the country was allowed 60 clothing coupons per year.

A man's coat took up 16 coupons, a pair of shoes another 5. Stockings were difficult to find, so many women darkened their legs with shoe polish and drew a line down the back of each leg to look like stocking seams.

By 1942 there were shortages of soap, and even water had to be used carefully. People were asked not to use more than 5 inches (12 cm) of water in their baths because the coal required to heat the water was needed even more for the weapons factories.

Everyone was urged to use less fuel in the home.

Wartime Food Rations for an Adult

Bacon and ham: 4 oz (100 g) per week
Meat: to the value of 1 shilling 2 pence (6p today) per week
Butter: 2 oz (50 g) per week
Cheese: 2 oz (50 g), sometimes it rose to 4 oz (100 g) per week
Margarine: 4 oz (100 g) per week
Cooking fat: 4 oz (100 g), often dropping to 2 oz (50 g) per week
Milk: 3 pints (1,800 ml) often dropping to 2 pints (1,200 ml) per week
Dried milk: one packet every 4 weeks
Sugar: 8 oz (225 g) per week
Preserves: 1 lb (450 g) every 2 months
Tea: 2 oz (50 g) per week
Eggs: 1 egg per week, sometimes dropping to 1 every 2 weeks
Dried eggs: one packet every 4 weeks
Sweets: 12 oz (350 g) every 4 weeks

We'll Eat Again: A Collection of Recipes from the War Years
by Marguerite Patten

The War Effort

In May 1940, Neville Chamberlain resigned as prime minister and Winston Churchill took over as the leader of a coalition government. The new government set up the Local Defence Volunteers, or 'Home Guard' as it became known, for those men between the ages of 17 and 65 who wanted to help defend their towns and villages in the event of a German invasion.

When it started, the Home Guard had no uniforms or weapons. Volunteers turned up with ancient shotguns or made do with knives fixed to metal poles or broom handles. Even when the men were given uniforms, they did not always fit properly. But belonging to the Home Guard meant that those men who were not able to join the armed forces could still help the war effort in an active way.

Members of the Home Guard being trained by a sergeant from the regular army. Notice that the men do not have uniforms.

Anyone who was not involved in the fighting was encouraged to help in the war effort in any way possible. Collecting salvage was one way in which everyone could do something.

Anything that could be re-used was collected in sacks and handed over to salvage collectors, who took it to the local collecting dump.

The War is driving Hitler back
But here's one way to win it.
Just give your salvage men the sack
And see there's plenty in it.
Popular song

The materials needed to make war weapons were salvaged from everyday items. Saucepans, kettles, tin baths, tin cans, railings and all kinds of scrap metal were collected.

Your railing will be melted down to make ships, shells, guns, tanks and aircraft, and thus will help win this war.
Ministry of Supply leaflet

This huge mountain of pots and pans was part of the 'Saucepans for Spitfires' campaign.

In truth, much of the metal collected during the war years remained in the scrapyard and was never used. But it must have made people very proud to watch a Spitfire or Hurricane flying overhead and think, 'perhaps my old saucepans are part of those planes'.

The Battle of Britain

In England they're filled with curiosity and keep asking 'Why doesn't he come?' Be calm. Be calm. He's coming! He's coming!

Adolf Hitler speaking at a rally on
4 September 1940

By June 1940, France had been defeated by the German army. Nearly a quarter of a million British troops fighting in France had been forced to retreat to the English Channel. They were successfully evacuated from the beaches at Dunkirk by warships and civilian boats, while under constant attack from the air.

Hitler knew that an invasion force heading for Britain would be bombed from the air, so he first had to destroy the Royal Air Force. August 1940 saw the beginning of what became known as the 'Battle of Britain'. Wave after wave of German bombers attacked ships in the Channel and dropped their bombs on southern coastal towns. When British fighter planes proved very successful in shooting down German aircraft, Hitler sent even larger forces to bomb the fighter aerodromes in the south-east.

This Italian wartime postcard celebrates the Italian–German alliance during the Battle of Britain.

Hurricane fighter pilots resting between combat flights.

Below A wartime poster with Winston Churchill's famous remark in praise of the brave fighter pilots who protected the country during the Battle of Britain.

People in the south could watch air battles going on over their heads as vapour trails twisted and criss-crossed the sky.

> *Games at school were liable to be enlivened by dog-fights between aircraft overhead and it was sometimes necessary to run for cover as a stream of bullets ploughed across the pitch.*
> Children of the Blitz *by Robert Westall*

During the Battle of Britain, air crews sometimes flew into action six or seven times a day. These exhausted and brave fighter pilots succeeded in defending Britain. When Hitler failed to win control of the skies by the late summer, he started to bomb the cities.

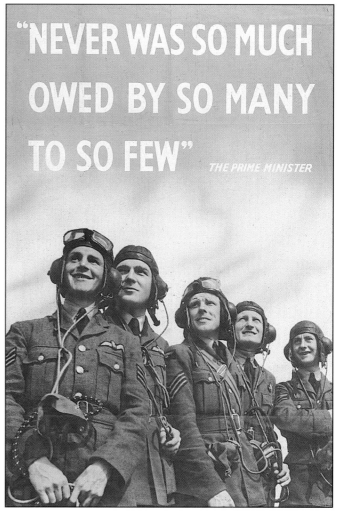

"NEVER WAS SO MUCH OWED BY SO MANY TO SO FEW" *THE PRIME MINISTER*

The Blitz on London

I see the damage done by the enemy . . . But I also see the spirit of an unconquerable people.
Winston Churchill, from *The Daily Herald*,
16 November 1940

The Blitz on Britain in 1940 and 1941 had two main aims: first, to destroy factories, oil depots and other places important for the war effort; second, to break the spirit of the British people so that they would be too tired and downhearted to fight back when the planned German invasion took place. But the Blitz failed to break morale; in fact, it did the opposite:

Balham High Road, London, after a bombing raid that destroyed houses and left an overturned bus perched on the edge of a bomb crater.

In every heart there is not fear, only a most passionate hatred of the enemy, and a determination to carry on at all costs.
Winston Churchill,
from *The Daily Herald*,
16 November 1940

No one was fully prepared for the huge amount of damage caused by the first bombing raids. Air Raid Precautions (ARP) workers struggled to clear away rubble and bring people to safety; firemen fought fire after fire; and hundreds were on the move, looking for safe places to live.

When the raid was over we could smell the burning and the sky was a huge red glow. It could be seen for miles that night and lit up the places like it was broad daylight.

Waiting for the All Clear
by Ben Wicks

Throughout the Blitz, bombs fell almost every night, and often during the daylight hours as well. Every area of the city was hit. But London was well defended. Anti-aircraft guns, searchlights and barrage balloons prevented the German planes from flying too low, making it difficult for the bombers to reach their targets.

Above   A view over ruins in inner London after a bomb attack.

Left   Barrage balloons prevented enemy planes from flying low over their targets. These barrage balloons are flying over Buckingham Palace.

The Blitz on other Cities

In the autumn of 1940, the Germans extended their bombing raids beyond the south-east and began to attack other major cities such as Birmingham, Southampton, Swansea and Coventry.

During the night of 14 November 1940, German bomber planes devastated Coventry. George VI visited the area and wrote in his diary:

Poor Coventry! I was horrified at the sight of the centre of the town . . . The water, electricity, and gas services had ceased to function . . . The people in the street wondered where they were . . . nothing could be recognized.

The remains of Coventry Cathedral after the bombing raid on the night of 14 November 1940, during which much of Coventry was destroyed.

Throughout the spring of 1941, there were heavy bombing raids in the West Midlands and on Merseyside. In March, the Germans turned their attention to Scotland. The shipyards and weapons factories at Clydebank in Glasgow were tempting targets; two heavy bombing raids on Clydebank resulted in almost total destruction. Of the 12,000 houses in the town, only 8 were left undamaged, and 55,000 people were made homeless.

Bombed tenement houses in Glasgow.

Wherever the bombs fell, there were also many brave deeds.

> *And my sister and I, we ran up into the house and there was an incendiary bomb blazing like mad in the middle of the couch. And she got the coal shovel and I got a basin and we lifted it into the basin and chucked it out the window. So that saved the house going on fire . . .*
> The Greenock Blitz (*Inverclyde District Libraries, 1991*)

A woman factory worker is rescued from the rubble following an air raid.

Sometimes it was not a whole fleet of German bombers but rather a single plane that caused terrible damage.

> *Lowestoft's worst raid was on a day of snow, just before dusk. One lone raider loomed out of cloud above the main street and dropped four bombs on to shops and a crowded restaurant. Seventy people were killed and more than a hundred injured. The individual dive-bomber made it seem much more personal – one enemy plane looking for someone to kill.*
> War Boy: A Country Childhood
> *by Michael Foreman*

Life in the Shelters

My father wouldn't have an air raid shelter. He said it would take up too much room in his garden . . . When the Blitz started we were all under the dining-room table complete with dog.

The Greenock Blitz *(Inverclyde District Libraries, 1991)*

Throughout the Blitz, people had to find shelter from the bombs. Anderson shelters were damp and often flooded in wet weather. The brick-built public shelters were drier but not always safe because nearby bomb blasts often caused roofs to shift and walls to collapse. But there were other places that offered shelter. Each evening, hundreds of Londoners took the train to the Chislehurst Caves, south-east of London, where they could sleep in safety; in Nottingham some people sheltered in caves beneath the town. In Northfleet, east of London, families set up home in the long tunnels linking chalk quarries. In Ramsgate, on the east coast, the people could shelter in purpose-built deep tunnels that had been completed just before the war began. Some families spent weeks at a time underground.

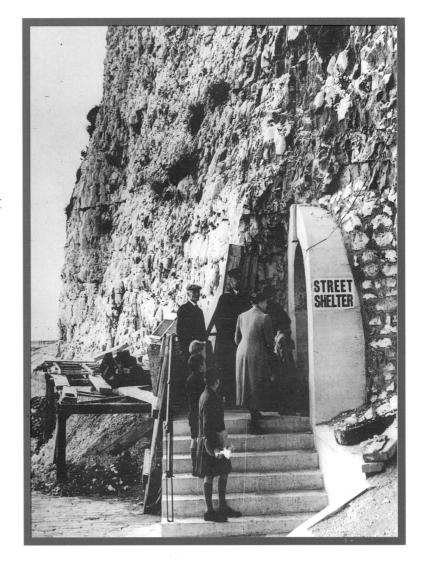

People entering the deep tunnels cut out of the chalk cliffs at Ramsgate, Kent. They would spend the night there, safe from the falling bombs.

This woman is reading a bedtime story to her seven children as she puts them to bed in an Anderson shelter.

My mother put curtains round the chalky walls and across the door to make it private and homely. We had lino on the floor. We had the cat and the budgie down there, and a radio.
Stories from the Past *edited by Brian Moses*

Thousands of Londoners found shelter in the underground train system, or tube. When the power was switched off at night, people slung hammocks across the track or bedded down in passageways, on platforms and even between the rails.

Londoners bedding down for the night in Aldwych tube station.

All over Britain, people tried to endure the air raids as best they could.

I was terrified but I had to be brave in front of the children . . . The raid went on for some time. I sang songs to the children and read story books just to keep their minds off it.
The Greenock Blitz
(Inverclyde District Libraries, 1991)

Wartime Entertainment

When war was declared, all theatres, cinemas and dance halls were immediately closed down. The government feared there would be great loss of life if bombs fell on such crowded places. But so many people complained about the closures that the places of entertainment were soon re-opened.

During the war years, most people visited the cinema at least once a week, trying to escape the hardships of war. The most popular wartime film was *Gone With the Wind*, a story of love and war during the American Civil War. *Tarzan*, *Flash Gordon* and *The Lone Ranger* were favourites at the Saturday morning picture shows for children.

Dance halls were always crowded. There were new wartime dances such as *The Blackout Stroll*, and new hit songs with wartime themes such as *The White Cliffs of Dover*, *We'll Meet Again*, *There'll Always Be an England* and *Run, Rabbit, Run*, which was changed to *Run, Adolf, Run*. The singer Vera Lynn gave courage to the troops with these songs. Her radio programme, *Sincerely Yours*, also featured song requests and messages for the men in the forces.

Troops begging autographs from 'Forces Sweetheart' Vera Lynn.

Singer and comedian George Formby entertaining tube shelterers.

The Entertainment National Service Association (ENSA) organized groups of singers, musicians actors and comedians to travel throughout the country and into the war zones entertaining the troops. ENSA also put on entertainment for the people sheltering in the tube during the Blitz.

There were comedy programmes on the radio to help brighten up people's lives. Every week about 16 million people tuned in to hear *ITMA (It's That Man Again)* with its cast of crazy characters that included Colonel Chinstrap, a German spy named Funf and Mrs Mopp the charlady. For children there was *Children's House* with Uncle Mac, who always finished his programme with the comforting phrase 'Goodnight Children, Everywhere'. The BBC news was especially important; families would gather round the radio at 9 o'clock each evening to learn how the war was going.

A family tunes into a news report on the radio. They have their gas masks ready in case of a poison gas raid.

Women at War

Going to work in a factory during the war was a wonderful experience. For the first time, I had some degree of freedom from my parents' control; I had money of my own to do with as I liked; and I was being given responsibilities and treated like an adult. I made lots of new friends at work – young women like myself who were having their first taste of freedom. We felt good about ourselves, and although there were terrible things going on all around us, the war years were the happiest time of our lives.

Dorothy Harris, personal
reminiscences

WOMEN OF BRITAIN
COME INTO
THE FACTORIES
ASK AT ANY EMPLOYMENT EXCHANGE FOR ADVICE AND FULL DETAILS

During the war many women took on jobs that previously had been done only by men. Women worked in shipyards, aircraft factories, engineering works, chemical plants and munitions factories. They became bus conductors, railway workers, labourers, welders and porters. By 1943, 9 out of 10 single women and 8 out of 10 married women were working in the armed forces or in industry. Although women did the same jobs as men, they earned only half as much as men did.

As more and more farm workers left the farms to join the armed forces or to take better paid jobs in the factories, new farm workers were badly needed.

This government poster urges women to take jobs in the factories. Throughout the war, women filled many of the jobs left vacant when the men went to fight. For many women this was the first time they had worked outside the home.

28

The Women's Land Army was set up to encourage women to work on the farms. It was extremely hard work, with low wages, long hours and few holidays. The 'Land Girls', as they became known, lived on the farms doing daily farm chores as well as ploughing, threshing, tree-felling and rat-catching.

Back to the land we must all lend a hand.
To the farms and the fields we must go.
There's a job to be done,
Though we can't fire a gun
We can still do our bit with the hoe . . .
                    The Land Army song

Above Women shipbuilders. Women took on jobs that before the war had been done only by men.

The Women's Voluntary Service (WVS) helped with the war effort in many ways – running canteens, bringing tea and blankets to bomb victims and helping with evacuation. One WVS member from Yorkshire managed to disarm and capture a German parachutist by threatening him with a pitchfork.

Auxiliary Territorial Service (ATS) students learning how to plot the course of enemy bombers. They would then pass on the information to gunsites, searchlights and other defence services.

Occupied Britain: The Channel Islands

The British government thought that the Germans would never invade the Channel Islands, so it withdrew all its troops in June 1940. However, Adolf Hitler considered the Channel Islands to be a threat to his control of France. He also wanted very much to put German troops on British soil.

Many islanders panicked when the British troops left. Arrangements were made for children to be evacuated to the mainland.

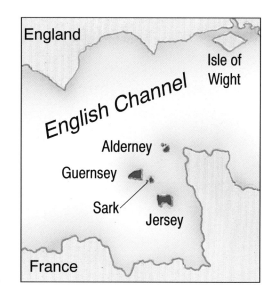

They were allowed to take only what they could carry, and so with gas-masks over their shoulders, and clutching an assortment of cases, carrier bags, favourite teddy bears, haversacks and the like, they stood in groups . . . all trying to show a brave face.

The Silent War *by Frank Falla*

A German victory march through the streets of St Peter Port, Guernsey.

On 28 June 1940, German planes dropped bombs on Guernsey and Jersey. Eight-year-old Molly Bihet, who was living in St Peter Port at the time, saw the planes coming in very low over the harbour.

We gave them a wave with a cucumber we'd just bought from a shop nearby but soon ran for shelter as they were German planes which started to machine gun and bomb the ships and the harbour.

A Child's War *by Molly Bihet*

Forty-four people died in the air raids, and many more were injured. The Germans met no resistance, and two days later they occupied Guernsey and Jersey, then moved on to Alderney and Sark.

The first Germans to arrive on the islands were in high spirits because they believed they would soon be occupying the rest of Britain. They were quite friendly with the islanders but warned them to obey all orders issued by the German authorities.

Above The captured British flag of Guernsey is about to be flown to Germany as a prize of war.

Below The German flag with the Swastika, the symbol of Hitler's Nazi party, flying over a building in occupied Jersey.

The Channel Islands under German Rule

One of the problems of life under German rule was the sheer monotony of existence. Day after day there was work, queuing for food or clothing, travelling only within designated areas, and no formal entertainment apart from what the Nazis approved.

Liberation *by Nick Machon*

The Germans took away the islanders' radios, and anyone caught with a radio or crystal set could be fined or imprisoned. One Jersey man and his son were sent to a German prison camp for having a radio, and they both died there.

Food was rationed, but by early 1941 finding enough food to eat was becoming a problem. One woman wrote in her diary:

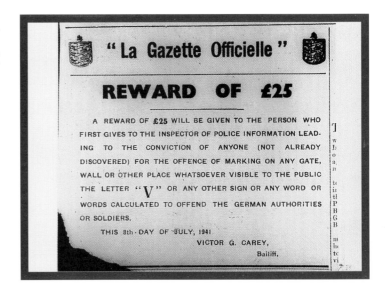

"La Gazette Officielle"

REWARD OF £25

A REWARD OF £25 WILL BE GIVEN TO THE PERSON WHO FIRST GIVES TO THE INSPECTOR OF POLICE INFORMATION LEADING TO THE CONVICTION OF ANYONE (NOT ALREADY DISCOVERED) FOR THE OFFENCE OF MARKING ON ANY GATE, WALL OR OTHER PLACE WHATSOEVER VISIBLE TO THE PUBLIC THE LETTER "V" OR ANY OTHER SIGN OR ANY WORD OR WORDS CALCULATED TO OFFEND THE GERMAN AUTHORITIES OR SOLDIERS.

THIS 8th DAY OF JULY, 1941.

VICTOR G. CAREY,
Bailiff.

February 1st 1941: Tea and cocoa have nearly all gone and they are making barley, parsnip and carrot coffee.
May 7th 1941: For two weeks there have been no joints of meat on sale.

Liberation *by Nick Machon*

The Germans were upset to see the letter V, which stood for Victory, being painted around the Channel Islands. They issued this warning in all the local newspapers.

Food, clothing and fuel became increasingly scarce. By 1944, both the Germans and the islanders were suffering from the shortages. A woman who was a child during the German occupation, remembers scrounging food from the Germans:

A German propaganda film showing at the Gaumont Palace, on Guernsey. The cinema was also used as an air-raid shelter.

We would pick up potatoes (mostly rotten) from the street while the Germans were unloading stores . . . One kind soldier filled my basket when the guard wasn't looking, but another one sometimes arrived – he had a whip to move us on – and he used it.

Liberation *by Nick Machon*

There were reports of islanders eating cats and dogs at times to ward off starvation. The situation was eased a little at the end of 1944 when ships carrying Red Cross parcels began to visit the islands.

Barbed wire around the harbour of St Peter Port, Guernsey. The Germans restricted access to the harbour.

Americans in Britain

The USA entered the
war in December
1941 after Japan,
which was one of
the Axis Powers,
bombed the
American naval
base at Pearl
Harbor, Hawaii.
The first American
soldiers and airmen
arrived in Britain at
the beginning of
1942.

An American soldier with
war orphans 'adopted' by
his unit.

American soldiers were known as GIs because their
equipment was labelled 'Government Issue'. They
were paid up to five times more than British troops
and were kept supplied with luxury goods from
home, such as fruit, chocolate, ice-cream, sweets,
butter, sugar and Coca-Cola. GIs also had lipstick,
perfume and nylon stockings to give away, so they
were popular with British women. After the war,
thousands of 'GI brides' left Britain to begin new
lives in the USA with their American husbands.

With the arrival of the GIs, many people became aware of American racism. Black GIs had to live apart from white soldiers in the army camp, and they were expected to visit different pubs, clubs and cafes. Many Britons were upset by this attitude. One newspaper assured all black Americans that 'there is no colour bar in this country.'

By the spring of 1944, there were over a million American troops in Britain, mostly in the south where plans for the invasion of France were well underway. 'D-Day', as the invasion became known, took place on 6 June 1944.

Above American GIs contributing their candy and gum rations to a Christmas fund for British children.

Left American soldiers in a military hospital join in a song with members of the ENSA entertainment group.

Wartime Childhood

For children who remained with their parents in the cities, there was the terror of the bombings, the sleepless nights huddled in air-raid shelters, and the loss of family members, friends and homes. Children were often told sad news about their friends when they returned to school.

When we went to school, the names would go up on the blackboard – all your friends that had been killed. We used to say a little prayer and hope it would be different the next night, but it wasn't.

A People's War *by Peter Lewis*

Above Wartime lessons for those who remained in the cities. Notice the gas mask on each boy's desk.

The number of children allowed in school at one time was limited by the size of the school's air-raid shelter – it had to be big enough to hold all of the students. Many children had lessons for only half a day, then changed places with other pupils. Education suffered as a result, and by the end of the war many children were behind in reading and writing.

Left A boy repairing his toy car does not seem to be bothered by the nearness of an unexploded bomb.

Children had lots of free time to roam the bombed streets and discover hiding places in the rubble. Another popular activity with children, but rather less so with adults, was collecting war souvenirs.

Chas had the second-best collection of war souvenirs in Yarmouth. It was all a matter of knowing where to look . . . The best places to look were where no one else would dream, like in the dry soil under privet hedges. You often found machine-gun bullets there, turned into little metal mushrooms as they hit the ground.

The Machine Gunners *by Robert Westall*

Those who stayed behind in the city lived with the dangers of bombing raids. This young boy from the East End of London wears a helmet as bomb protection.

The Doodlebug Menace

A week after the successful D-Day invasion into France, Hitler launched his secret weapon – the V1 aeroplane – against Britain. The V1, known as the 'flying bomb' or the 'doodlebug', was a pilotless plane carrying high explosives. When a doodlebug ran out of fuel, it would fall from the sky, blowing up as it hit the ground.

By 16 June, the Germans were launching up to 73 doodlebugs a day against Britain. London, Kent and Sussex, which were closest to the launch sites in France, were the hardest hit, and the area became known as 'Bomb Alley'. But occasionally doodlebugs would land as far away as Nottinghamshire and Yorkshire.

LEAVE THIS TO US SONNY — YOU OUGHT TO BE OUT OF LONDON

MINISTRY OF HEALTH EVACUATION SCHEME

The people of Britain had hoped that the D-Day landings in France would soon bring victory and an end to the war, so these fresh bomb attacks were a great blow to morale. The flying bombs were a terrible menace. They threatened everyone and everything in their path. The writer Evelyn Waugh compared them to

> *. . . a plague, as though the city were infected with enormous venomous insects.*
>
> Unconditional Surrender *by Evelyn Waugh*

When the doodlebugs started to fall on London, the government once again tried to encourage parents to send their children away to the safety of the countryside. In 1944, over a million women, children, elderly and disabled people left London and other citiies for 'safe' areas.

The flying bombs were attacked by British anti-aircraft guns and fighter planes.

The doodlebug at least gave some warning of its approach – when the plane's engine cut out, people knew it was about to come down. In September 1944, the V1 aeroplane was replaced with the V2 rocket, which gave no warning whatsoever. The worst V2 disaster was in Deptford, south of London, when a bomb landed on a Woolworths store packed with shoppers. The only way to stop the V2 rockets was to bomb or capture the launch sites.

Above Flying bomb damage in Islington, London.

Below A German V2 rocket being fuelled for an attack on Britain.

The End of the War

Throughout the bitterly cold winter of 1944–5, people were still queueing for food and suffering from shortages of fuel. However, there were some encouraging changes – the blackout gave way to a 'dim-out' and cars no longer needed masked headlights – but the war still went on.

Eager soldiers pulling copies of *The Stars and Stripes* from the press of the *London Times* at 9 pm on 7 May 1945, when an extra edition was printed to announce the news of Germany's surrender.

On the western front, the Allies were driving Hitler's army out of the countries it had invaded and back into Germany. In the east, Soviet troops were pushing the Germans out of the USSR and eastern Europe. Finally, on 25 April 1945, Soviet and American soldiers met south of Berlin in Germany.

People now believed the end was in sight and there was a great rush to buy flags and decorations for the victory celebrations. On 1 May 1945, news came through that Adolf Hitler had shot himself. News was also coming through of the concentration camps in which over six million people had died.

Photographs showing the horrors of these camps proved beyond doubt that the struggle to defeat Hitler had been a just one.

Germany surrendered in the first week of May. VE-Day – Victory in Europe – was declared on 8 May and celebrated by millions. Everywhere, there were street parties, bonfires, fireworks, music and flags.

On the Channel Islands, 9 May was Liberation Day. The Germans surrendered and British troops landed. Here is one woman's memory of that day:

Above Thousands of people gathered at Trafalgar Square in London to celebrate VE Day on 8 May 1945.

Below Liberation Day in the Channel Islands.

Returning Home

Left A newly-built aluminium prefab, one of many built on this housing estate in Surrey after the war had ended.

Below Villagers say goodbye to evacuees who are on their way back to London after the war. Many foster parents found it difficult to part with the children they had taken care of during the war years.

Many evacuees started returning home after September 1944. But others had to stay in the country-side until long after the war in Europe had ended because of the shortage of housing in bombed-out cities. Thousands of prefabricated houses, or 'prefabs', were built to help solve the housing problem.

It was often very difficult for foster parents to part with the children they had grown to love. Some children returning to homes where there was little affection ran away and tried to get back to their foster parents. Evacuees whose parents had been killed were sometimes adopted by their foster parents.

Those children who had spent the war years overseas in countries where there were no shortages found it particularly hard to adjust to life back home where food was still rationed. Many of these children had not seen their parents since they left Britain at the start of the war.

British teenagers arriving back from Australia after the war. For many, this would be the first time they had seen their parents since the start of the war.

Rusty was standing in the crowd on the quayside, when suddenly she found herself being hugged tightly by a woman in her thirties, dressed in green. After a few seconds Rusty realized that the woman was her mother . . . Rusty couldn't help staring at the woman's face. It was the first time in five years that she had seen it.

Back Home *by Michelle Magorian*

Gradually, nearly two million soldiers, sailors and airmen were demobbed. Many came home to meet children who only knew 'dad' as a photograph.

The war had altered people's lives in a great many ways. Some suffered from ill-health for the rest of their lives; many people had lost loved ones; many marriages had broken down during the war years. But there was also hope for the future.

I thought of those who had been dear to us who had not lived to see this . . . and then went indoors to stand looking at the sleeping faces of my two little sons, whose lives lay before them in a world of peace.

We'll Meet Again *by Vera Lynn with Robin Cross and Jenny de Gex*

Aftermath

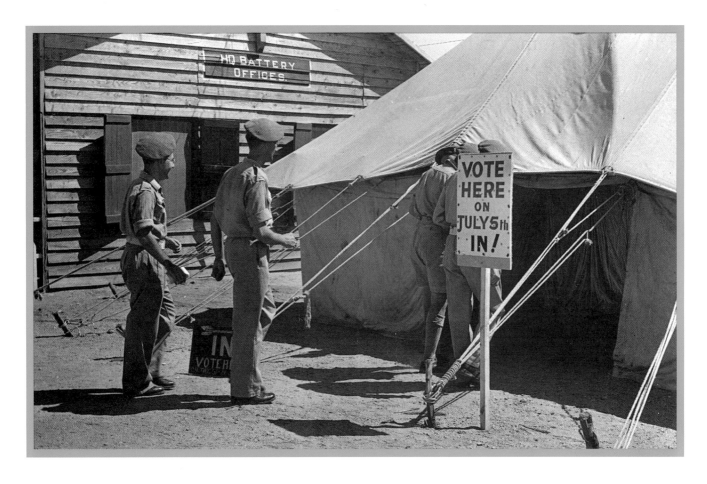

On 5 July 1945, a general election was held in Britain. Winston Churchill, the leader of the Conservative Party, stood against Clement Attlee, leader of the Labour Party. Attlee and his party won the election. Although Churchill had been an extremely popular wartime leader, the Labour Party won because it promised to set up the Welfare State to help reduce the terrible poverty that had been revealed during the war years.

The great expense of fighting the war had left Britain with very little money to rebuild bomb-damaged cities and ports. Rationing continued for several years after the war; at one stage, even bread and potatoes were rationed.

Soldiers voting on 5 July 1945 at a polling station in the Royal Engineers Base Depot near Cairo, Egypt. Servicemen who were stationed abroad were able to vote by post in the 1945 election.

The war against Japan continued until the USA dropped two atomic bombs on the Japanese cities of Hiroshima and Nagasaki. Japan surrendered within the week, and 15 August 1945 was celebrated as VJ Day – Victory in Japan. A Liverpool businessman noted in his diary:

There were no signs of joy, of enthusiasm, no cheering crowds, all shops shut and the streets almost deserted . . . I feel no elation, no uplifting of the spirit, only a sort of dumb inarticulate thankfulness that the hell of war, the killing, the misery is over.

We'll Meet Again *by Vera Lynn, with Robin Cross and Jenny de Gex*

Above Prime Minster Clement Attlee walks in procession with the former prime minister, Winston Churchill, on VJ Day, 15 August 1945.

Below A queue for meat outside a butcher's shop in Portobello Road, London, in April 1949.

Glossary

All clear   The sound made by a siren to show that it was safe for people to come out of their air-raid shelters.

Allies   The countries that fought together against Germany, Italy and Japan (the Axis Powers) during the Second World War. The major Allied countries were Britain, the USA and the USSR.

Anti-aircraft guns   Guns used against enemy aircraft.

Axis Powers   The three countries – Germany, Italy and Japan – that fought together against the Allies during the Second World War.

Barrage balloons   Huge balloons winched up into the sky to ward off attacks by low-flying aircraft.

Call up   An order from the government to join the armed forces.

Charlady   A cleaning woman who works in a private house.

Civil defence   The organization of non-military citizens to protect their country and their homes against attack from enemy forces.

Civilian   Not part of the armed forces or the police force.

Coalition government   A government formed by the temporary coalition (joining together) of political parties.

Concentration camp   A camp where Jews and political prisoners were imprisoned during the war; most prisoners did not survive the harsh conditions in the concentration camps.

Corrugated iron   A sheet of iron that has been formed into regular folds and grooves to give added strength.

Crystal set   Home-made radio set.

Demobbed   Short for demobilized, which means to be released from military service.

Designated   A specified, or specially named, place or thing.

Evacuation   The removal of people from a dangerous place to a safer place.

Evacuees   People who have been evacuated from their homes.

Foster parents   People who take in a child and looked after him or her as part of their own family.

Inarticulate   Unable to express yourself well in speech.

Incendiary   A small bomb that starts a fire when it explodes.

Journalist   Someone who writes for a newspaper or a magazine.

Liberation   Set free from enemy occupation.

Masked headlight   A headlight with a covering that allowed only a slit of light to show through.

Morale   A person's state of mind with regard to courage and hopefulness. If your morale is low, you feel depressed and discouraged; if your morale is high, you feel courageous and hopeful.

Munitions   Shells and bullets for guns.

Precautions   Actions taken beforehand to prevent damage or injury.

Prefabricated   Made beforehand. Prefabricated buildings are made in sections in factories and put together on site.

Propaganda   The promotion of a particular set of ideas or beliefs to support one's cause or to discredit an opponent's cause.

Ration   To limit the amount of food, clothing, etc. that a person is allowed to buy.

Racism   The practice of treating people as inferior because they belong to a different race.

Resistance   Opposing or fighting against the authority of an occupying enemy.

Salvage   To save and re-use waste goods and materials.

Scabies   A skin disease that causes itching.

Searchlight   A light with a strong beam that can track enemy aircraft.

Siren   A device that makes a loud hooting or wailing noise as a warning signal.

Tenement   A run-down building with many flats in the poorer parts of large cities.

U-boat   A German submarine.
USSR   Union of Soviet Socialist Republics. The USSR was made up of 15 republics that in 1992 split up into individual, independent countries.
Venomous   Poisonous.
Volunteers   People who do jobs without pay.

Welfare State   A system of running a country whereby the government looks after the well-being of the citizens by providing social services such as medical care.
Wireless   A radio. The first radios were called wireless sets because they were the first machines that could send messages on radio waves rather than along wires.

Books to Read

Growing up at War by Maureen Hill (Armada/Collins, 1989)
Children of the Blitz: Memoirs of Wartime Childhood by Robert Westall (Penguin Books, 1987)
How We Used to Live by Freda Kelsall (Macdonald/Yorkshire TV, 1987)
The Home Front by Stewart Ross (Wayland, 1990)
The Home Front series: The Home Front 1939-1945; The Blitz; Evacuation; Prisoners of War; Rationing; Propaganda, Women's War both by Fiona Reynoldson (Wayland, 1991)

Acknowledgements

Grateful acknowledgement is given for permission to reprint copyright material:
Page 5 *The Day War Broke Out* by Peter Haining (W. H. Allen and Co, 1989)
Pages 8, 9, 11 *No Time to Say Goodbye* by Ben Wicks (Bloomsbury, 1986)
Page 10 *The World Is a Wedding* by Bernard Kops (Valentine, Mitchell and Co, 1973)
Pages 13, 23, 34 *War Boy: A Country Childhood* by Michael Foreman (Pavilion Books, 1989)
Page 15 *We'll Eat Again: A Collection of Recipes from the War Years* by Marguerite Patten (Hamlyn, 1985)
Page 19 *Children of the Blitz* by Robert Westall (Penguin, 1987)
Page 21 *Waiting for the All Clear* by Ben Wicks (Bloomsbury, 1990)
Pages 23, 24, 25 *The Greenock Blitz* (Inverclyde District Libraries, 1991)
Page 25 *Stories from the Past* edited by Brian Moses (Scholastic, 1994)
Page 30 *The Silent War* by Frank Falla (Burbridge Ltd, 1967)
Page 31 *A Child's War* by Molly Bihet (Private publication)
Pages 32, 33, 41 *Liberation* by Nick Machon (The Guernsey Press, 1985)
Page 36 *A People's War* by Peter Lewis (Methuen, 1986)
Page 37 *The Machine Gunners* by Robert Westall (Macmillan, 1975)
Page 38 *Unconditional Surrender* by Evelyn Waugh (Chapman and Hall, 1961)
Page 39 *Thanet at War: 1939–45* by Roy Humphreys (Alan Sutton Publishing, 1991)
Page 43 *Back Home* by Michelle Magonian (Viking, 1985)
Page 43 *We'll Meet Again* by Vera Lynn with Robin Cross and Jenny De Gex (Sidgwick and Jackson, 1989)
While every effort has been made to trace copyright holders, the Publishers apologize for any inadvertent omissions.

Index

Entries in bold refer to the pictures.